SOCIAL
MEDIA
SENSATIONS

Snapchat

Madeleine R. Spalding

**Checkerboard
Library**

An Imprint of Abdo Publishing
abdopublishing.com

abdopublishing.com

Published by Abdo Publishing, a division of ABDO, PO Box 398166, Minneapolis, Minnesota 55439. Copyright © 2017 by Abdo Consulting Group, Inc. International copyrights reserved in all countries. No part of this book may be reproduced in any form without written permission from the publisher. Checkerboard Library™ is a trademark and logo of Abdo Publishing.

Printed in the United States of America, North Mankato, Minnesota
062016
092016

THIS BOOK CONTAINS
RECYCLED MATERIALS

Design: Emily Love, Mighty Media, Inc.
Production: Mighty Media, Inc.
Editor: Liz Salzmann
Cover Photos: Getty Images, iStockphoto, Shutterstock
Interior Photos: AP Images, pp. 5, 15, 21; Getty Images, pp. 11, 13, 19, 24;
iStockphoto, pp. 9, 27; Shutterstock, pp. 4, 7, 12-13, 16, 23, 25, 29

Publishers Cataloging-in-Publication Data
Names: Spalding, Madeleine R., author.
Title: Snapchat / by Madeleine R. Spalding.
Description: Minneapolis, MN : Abdo Publishing, [2017] | Series: Social media
    sensations | Includes index.
Identifiers: LCCN 2016934276 | ISBN 9781680781922 (lib. bdg.) |
    ISBN 9781680775778 (ebook)
Subjects: LCSH: Snapchat--Juvenile literature. | Photography--Digital techniques-
    -Juvenile literature. | Image processing--Digital techniques--Juvenile literature.
    | Internet industry--United States--Juvenile literature. | Online social networks-
    -Juvenile literature.
Classification: DDC 775--dc23
LC record available at /http://lccn.loc.gov/2016934276

Contents

Snapchat

URL: https://www.snapchat.com

PURPOSE: Snapchat is a photo- and video-sharing app. The images disappear after being viewed.

CURRENT CEO: Evan Spiegel

NUMBER OF USERS: About 200 million

JULY 2011
Picaboo is launched

SEPTEMBER 2011
Picaboo is renamed Snapchat

NOVEMBER 2014
Spiegel and Murphy turn down Facebook's offer to buy Snapchat

SEPTEMBER 2015
Snapchat introduces the Lenses feature

Meet the Founders

EVAN THOMAS SPIEGEL was born in Los Angeles, California. He went to college at Stanford University in California, where he met Snapchat cofounders Bobby Murphy and Frank Brown. Spiegel is Snapchat's Chief Executive Officer.

BOBBY MURPHY was born in Berkeley, California. Before cofounding Snapchat in 2011, Murphy studied at Stanford University. He is the Chief Technology Officer of Snapchat.

FRANK REGINALD "REGGIE" BROWN lived in South Carolina before attending Stanford University. He cofounded Snapchat, but was no longer with the company one month after its launch.

Evan Spiegel   Bobby Murphy

CHAPTER 1

What Is Snapchat?

Your smartphone beeps. It's a snap from your friend! You open Snapchat. You tap your friend's name to view her message. She appears making a funny face. You laugh as the image disappears. You quickly take a selfie making a funny face and send it to your friend. In seconds, you see that she's viewed it! This is the magic of Snapchat.

Snapchat is a social media app for smartphones and tablets. The app uses the device's camera. Friends find each other by name or phone number. Then they send each other photos and short videos, called snaps.

Users can draw on and add text and filters to their images. These include the time, emoticons, and other fun features.

Did You Know?

In July 2015, Ireland had more Snapchat users than any other country.

Many people use Snapchat to take fun photos, such as selfies with a pet.

Once a snap is created and sent, it can only be viewed for a few seconds. Then the image disappears. This allows users to share images without using up their mobile device's storage. They can instantly share moments with friends. Snapchat connects users around the world one quick photo at a time.

CHAPTER 2

From Idea to App

Snapchat began as a class project. In April 2011, Evan Spiegel and Frank Reginald "Reggie" Brown were students at Stanford University in California. The pair teamed up for a final class project of creating an original product.

Brown had an idea. People sometimes post photos on social media that they later wish they hadn't. While people can delete their posts, their photos may have already been downloaded by others. The original poster has no way to delete those copies. Brown wished there was a way to send photos that would disappear after being viewed.

Spiegel and Brown wanted to solve this problem. They decided to create an app that automatically deletes photos after they are viewed. This way, users wouldn't have to worry about copies of their photos being on the Internet forever.

Spiegel and Brown asked Stanford graduate Bobby Murphy to help create the app. The trio worked for months. Finally, the app was ready. Its creators named it Picaboo, after the word "peek," meaning a quick look. Its logo was a ghost, relating to "boo" in the name.

Picaboo was launched on July 13, 2011. But not many people downloaded it. By that fall, Picaboo had only 127 users. Its founders knew something had to change.

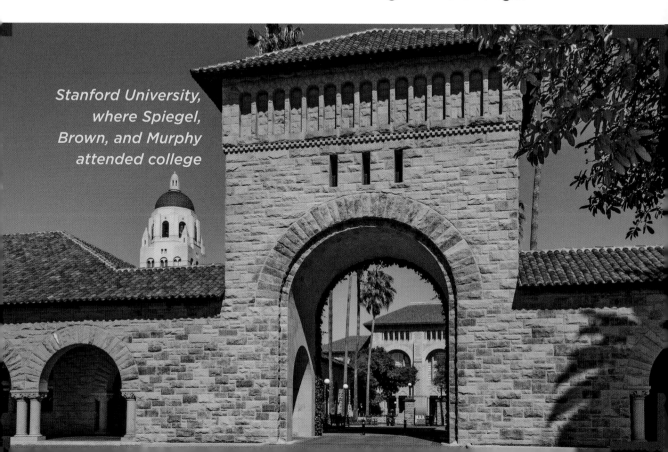

Stanford University, where Spiegel, Brown, and Murphy attended college

CHAPTER 3

Snapchat Is Born

Picaboo's three founders worked hard to make their new app successful the summer of its launch. Still, their user base hadn't grown. Soon the relationship between the three friends grew tense.

Spiegel, Brown, and Murphy argued over how much of the company each had a right to own. Brown said he had come up with the idea, name, and logo for Picaboo. He also helped market the app. For these reasons, he wanted to own 30 percent of the company. But Spiegel and Murphy didn't think Brown's contributions were that important. They forced him out of the company.

Meanwhile, in the fall of 2011, Murphy and Spiegel had received a letter from a photo-book company. The company was also called Picaboo, and it owned the rights to the name. Murphy and Spiegel were going to have to rename their app.

Snapchat's early headquarters near Venice Beach in Los Angeles, California

Murphy and Spiegel didn't see renaming Picaboo as a **setback**. They thought a new start might be good for their app. The pair chose the name Snapchat, after the action of snapping a photo.

CHAPTER 4

Snapchat at School

Soon after its name change, Snapchat got a boost in popularity. High school students in California took notice of the app. Schools there gave students tablets to use for assignments. Teachers didn't want students using social media at school. So apps such as Facebook were banned on these devices. But school administrators were unaware of Snapchat, so it wasn't banned.

Students began using Snapchat during school. It allowed them to

High school students' use of Snapchat led to its user base growing to 30,000 by early 2012.

send messages, soon known as snaps, during class. And there was no evidence left behind. Word of Snapchat spread. Soon, teenagers all over the country were using Snapchat.

Disappearing Snaps

When someone sends a snap, they set a timer. It limits how long the snap will be visible to the recipient upon opening. This can be between one and ten seconds. After a user hits send, the image goes to Snapchat's servers, and then to the recipient. The recipient taps on the snap to view it. This starts the timer. When the set time is up, the servers delete the snap.

CHAPTER 5

Attracting Investors

As Snapchat's popularity continued to rise with students, the app's user base grew by the thousands. By April 2012, there were more than 100,000 users. But the company had yet to make a profit. In fact, Spiegel and Murphy were losing money.

Snapchat is a free app. But it costs money to run the service. The company has to pay for servers used to store user information and transfer the snaps. As the number of Snapchat users grew, the company needed more servers. The founders needed more money to buy this equipment.

Spiegel borrowed money from family. And Murphy paid his share from money he made at another job. But it wasn't enough. Spiegel and Murphy needed help.

The headquarters of Alibaba Group in Hangzhou, China. This Internet company invested $200 million in Snapchat in 2015.

Luckily, investors were beginning to notice Snapchat. They knew the app was growing in popularity. Many believed it could become as successful as other social media companies.

Snapchat received its first investment in April 2012. A company called Lightspeed Venture Partners gave the company nearly $500,000. When Spiegel got the news, he dropped out of college. He couldn't wait to focus on growing the company.

CHAPTER 6

Keeping Snapchat

Investors weren't the only ones noticing Snapchat's growing popularity. So were competitors. One was Facebook founder Mark Zuckerberg.

In December 2012, Facebook released an app called Poke. It was designed to provide a service

Like the Snapchat founders, Mark Zuckerberg started his social media company, Facebook, when he was in college.

similar to Snapchat. But the app failed.

One reason Poke failed was Facebook's demographics. Many young people view Facebook as uncool. The site's users on average are older than Snapchat's users. After Poke's release, it was discovered that these older users were generally less interested in sending disappearing photos.

Facebook shut down Poke in May 2014. Six months after closing his app, Zuckerberg met with Spiegel and Murphy. He offered to buy Snapchat for $3 billion. But Spiegel and Murphy had put a lot of work into their company. They weren't willing to give Snapchat up. The founders declined Zuckerberg's offer.

CHAPTER 7

Snapchat Stories

After committing to keeping Snapchat, the founders decided to work on improving the app. They began adding new features. One was video snaps, added in December 2012. In addition to photos, users could now send each other videos that were up to 10 seconds long.

Snapchat Stories was another new feature. It was introduced in October 2013, and later renamed My Story. My Story allows a user to string several snaps together. Together, these snaps create a story. Snaps in the user's My Story disappear after 24 hours.

In June 2014, Snapchat introduced Our Story. This feature allowed users at the same location or event to add snaps to a shared story. The Snapchat team chooses topics for these stories. It also selects the best snaps to

The first Live Story was from a music festival in Las Vegas, Nevada. The festival was called the Electric Daisy Carnival.

include in each. The result is a story of the location or event that can be viewed by all Snapchat users. So, those not able to witness something live can still experience what it was like.

This new feature was later renamed Live Story. Most Live Stories are one to five minutes long. As with My Stories, snaps in Live Stories disappear after 24 hours.

CHAPTER 8

Politics and News

Snapchat connects users around the world with its fun features. But the app is also used for other purposes. Many politicians use social media to gain voter support.

Candidates for the 2016 US presidential election felt Snapchat could help them reach younger voters. These candidates shared their Snapchat usernames with the public. They asked people to follow them on the app. They used Snapchat to interact with their supporters.

A few candidates used Snapchat's Live Story feature to connect with voters. They asked Snapchat to create Live Stories of their campaign events. Hillary Clinton and Jeb Bush were two candidates who did this. Snapchat also broadcast Live Stories of presidential debates.

In addition to politics, Snapchat users can also keep up on news using the app. In January 2015, Snapchat launched its Discover feature. It lets news and information

Ten Republican presidential candidates participated in a debate on August 6, 2015. The Snapchat Live Story of the debate was very popular with people younger than 25.

outlets post content to Snapchat. This content can be seen by all Snapchat users. Discover stories change every 24 hours, so users know the content is up to date.

CHAPTER 9

Social Impact

Snapchat created Live Story to connect users around the world. Live Stories can also call attention to important world events and social causes. Two Live Stories in the summer of 2015 did just that.

On June 26, 2015, the Supreme Court legalized same-sex marriage in every US state. Many people across the United States celebrated the decision. Snapchat created a Live Story of the event.

People across the nation contributed to the Snapchat Live Story. They uploaded photos and videos of themselves smiling, hugging, and cheering. Snapchat users worldwide were able to share in US users' experience through this Live Story.

The following month, millions of Muslims were celebrating the religious holiday Ramadan in Mecca, Saudi Arabia. Snapchat created a Live Story for the event.

During Ramadan, pilgrims walk around the Kaaba. The Kaaba is a building in the mosque Al-Masjid al-Haram in Mecca.

Many participants uploaded photos and videos of their surroundings and the holiday's activities. This Live Story encouraged people worldwide to view the important religious event.

CHAPTER 10

Constant Change

Live Story greatly affected the type of content on Snapchat. But it is not the only big change. The Snapchat team is always thinking of ways to improve the app. Two recent features provided users new ways to connect.

A Snapchat Snapcode

☺ Added Me

○⁺ Add Friends

In May 2015, Snapchat added Snapcodes. A Snapcode is a Snapchat logo with a unique arrangement of dots on it. Every Snapchat user has his or her own code.

To add a friend by Snapcode, a user takes a photo of his or her Snapcode. Snapchat can also scan a photo of a Snapcode that has been sent to a user. In both instances, the user is prompted to add the new friend once the image is processed.

Another new feature is Add Nearby. It was introduced in July 2015. This feature provides a user a list of people near them who also have Add Nearby open. To add friends, the user can just tap on their names.

The Add Nearby feature makes it easier to find other Snapchat users.

In addition to new ways to connect, Snapchat has also introduced fun additions to its filter options. One is Lenses, added in September 2015. It allows users to add funny elements to snaps that contain images of people.

Lens options change often. A common type of lens makes it appear as though objects, such as rainbows, are shooting out of someone's eyes or mouth. The feature scans an image to locate the subject's eyes and mouth. Then it alters those facial features by adding images or changing their size.

Snapchat's changing features are just part of what makes the app fun for users. The app's disappearing photos and updated Live Stories mean its content is always changing. There are sure to be more changes to Snapchat in the future. But it will continue to connect people in an instant, and allow them to share in moments from around the world.

Adding fun features and lenses to already silly selfies and group shots is popular on Snapchat.

Snapchat

A Snapchat user must be at least 13 to have an account.

Snapchat can only be downloaded on a smartphone or tablet.

Opening Snapchat opens the camera on the user's device. To take a photo, the user presses the round button on the screen. They press and hold the button to take a video.

The buttons at the top of the screen are used to edit a photo. This includes adding text and drawing. The buttons at the bottom of the screen allow users to add filters and send their snaps to friends.

Users can view Live Stories by swiping left on the camera screen.

Snapchat's privacy settings allow users to choose which friends can see a My Story.

It is important people are safe when using Snapchat. They should never share personal information such as their home address in their snaps.

Glossary

administrator – a person who manages an operation, a department, or an office.

automatic – moving or acting by itself.

debate – a discussion or an argument.

delete – to remove or eliminate.

demographics – the qualities (such as age, sex, and income) of a specific group of people.

download – to transfer data from a computer network to a single computer or device.

emoticon – a small image of a face expressing some emotion, used in e-mail and apps to communicate a feeling or attitude.

filter – a tool that can change the appearance of a photo.

mobile – capable of moving or being moved.

recipient – someone who receives something.

selfie – an image of oneself taken by oneself using a digital camera, especially for posting on social networks.

server – a computer in a network that is used to provide services to other computers.

setback – a problem that causes delays or halts progress.

Supreme Court – the highest, most powerful court in the United States.

swipe – to drag one or more fingers across the screen of a smartphone or tablet.

technology – the science of how something works.

unique (yoo-NEEK) – being the only one of its kind.

update – to provide new or current information about something.

upload – to transfer data from a computer to a larger network.

Websites

To learn more about Social Media Sensations, visit booklinks.abdopublishing.com. These links are routinely monitored and updated to provide the most current information available.

Index